SEASONS IN HAIKU

by

Kathryn Waddell Takara

"A Spring Wind moves to dance
Any branch that isn't dead."

RUMI

Copyright @2022 Kathryn Waddell Takara
Pacific Raven Press LLC

ISBN   978-17367287-2-7 (print book)
ISBN   978-17367287-0-3 (ebook)

Cover Design by Jonathan Zane
Art work by Jonathan Zane
Graphics and Layout Design by Eien Design Studio

Editors – Allison Francis, Kathryn Takara
Contributing Editors – Karla Brundage, Alexandra Avery

Published by Pacific Raven Press, LLC

Licensed by Pacific Raven Press, LLC

Library of Congress Cataloging in Publication Catalogue as: Poetry, Haiku, Hawaii, History, Culture, African American

Pacific Raven Press is an Independent publisher
Published in the United States of America

Contact:

Pacific Raven Press, LLC
PO Box 678 Ka'a'awa, HI 96730

Telephone: 808-228-1630
FAX: 808-237-8974

Email: kathryn.takara@gmail.com
Website: www.pacificravenpress.co/

OTHER BOOKS BY THIS AUTHOR

Red Dreams Volcano Visions

Footprints Wings Phantasms

Shadow Dancing: $elling $urvival in China

Zimbabwe Spin: Politics and Poetics

Love's Seasons: Generations Genetics Myths

Timmy Turtle Teaches

Frank Marshall Davis:
The Fire and the Phoenix (Critical Biography)

Tourmalines: Beyond the Ebony Portal

Pacific Raven: Hawai`i Poems

New and Collected Poems

Oral Histories of African Americans

DEDICATION

To the Muse of Simplicity in Seeing

ACKNOWLEDGMENTS

I was inspired to complete this book project after I read Richard Wright's collection *Haiku: The Last Poems of an American Icon*. Wright's volume of almost 1000 Haiku was brilliantly discussed in the Afterword by Yoshinobu Hakutani and Robert L. Tener, which made my commitment to publishing my *Seasons in Haiku* so much stronger.

I extend my gratitude to my professional helpers in this project who are many, including editor, Allison Francis, and contributing editors, Karla Brundage, Rebekah Luke and Alexandra Avery; Liza Simon, writer; Sharon Yarbrough, my typist; and the ever-creative and gifted graphic designer and artist, Jonathan Zane. I acknowledge the original *Honolulu Advertiser* and *Star Bulletin* that published my haiku in the newspapers more than three decades ago.

I give a heartfelt shout out to my creative friends and supportive friends and loved ones in Hawai'i, California, China, and beyond who have encouraged me through the years in my quest to create and publish my poetry. These unnamed and treasured friends have and continue to inspire me, to take the time to read my work, offering valuable and perceptive, if informal, feedback. All of my friends in the arts, Ishmael Reed, Richard Hamasaki, Adela Chu, Sequoia, and Skytars, to mention a few, have been supportive in sharing their time, music, dance, and love with me. Most have attended or participated in my public events, book signings, and encouraged my best dreams and most private tender aspirations to manifest.

I would like to offer my appreciation for, and affiliation

with, various groups and associations that have offered me opportunities for new friendships, service, creative stimulation, and various platforms to share my work: my community sisters in public service, Pen Women (NLAPW); the Honolulu Chapter of The Links, Inc.; my book club, Bookies; Sharon Yarbrough (Sisters Empowering Hawai'i); various online poetry groups, national and international; the Knights of St. John, Russian Grand Priory, and Countess Tatiana Bobrinskoy, for her tireless leadership, encouragement, compassion and inspiration.

I celebrate my Ka'a'awa friends and neighbors for their belief in me, and their warm and loyal support through the decades. They have dared me to sing my insights using the power of poetry, informally listening to and enjoying the simplicity and complexity of haiku.

Various unnamed guides, teachers and professors also deserve recognition for expanding priorities, awareness, and critical thinking; including the psychology and practices of Gurdjieff and Ouspensky and other great teachers and leaders who have aided in my development of conscience, philosophies and understanding that I express my awakening on the path of mindfulness, and my growth toward consciousness, which I express in my writing.

Last, but not least, I am grateful to the ancestors, my husband Harvey Takara, my daughters Karla Brundage and Natasha Harrington, granddaughter Asha Brundage-Moore, son-in-law Brad Harrington and the younger grandchildren, Makayla, Zachary, and Mia, for their loving and constant support through the years, and with whom I have shared my experiences and memories transformed into poetry.

INTRODUCTION

A Graceful Provocation of Poetic Imagination

By Liza Simon

My first encounter with the poetry of Kathryn Waddell Takara was not on the written page, but on the stage of Pink's Garage, a nightclub housed inside a converted Honolulu warehouse. Rap and reggae by local bands comprised the usual fare in this funky venue. It was the mid-1990's and poetry had not yet arrived, as it has today, as a fashionably hip art form, amplified across the globe by social media. Notwithstanding beat poetry and a few other renegade genres, poetry bore the brand of a leisure pursuit preserved on a Eurocentric pedestal reserved for elitist literati minds.

Enter Kathryn Takara with an enormous tropical flower in her hair, and an equally vibrant and winning smile. That night in Pink's Garage, she had come not only to recite, but to conjure. Drawn from memory and leavened with sly and sophisticated commentary, she reeled out the spirited imagery of her life story, beginning with her African and Cherokee ancestral roots, continuing through her upbringing in rural Alabama amid the Jim Crow South, East and West Coast education, winding through her decades-long journey as a college professor, and culminating with her open-ended surrender to the wiles of island life in Hawai'i—destined to be her adopted home.

As singular as this narrative could have been, Takara made sure this was not the case. Despite the gravitas of her poetry, Takara's delivery felt cozy, confident and homespun--as if she were Anansi, the spider character of West African folktales, weaving all of us in the audience with threads of earnest emotion emanating from each poem. Things began to really percolate when Takara welcomed to the stage dancer Adela Chu and drummer Sango--two preeminent, Hawai'i-based performing artists, who fleshed out her words with contagious Caribbean-inflected body movement, and percussion.

The audience clapped and laughed in a steady flow of call and response. When the house lights finally went up, we were not ready to leave, and neither was Takara. She pulled up a chair, and we lingered together in animated cross currents of conversation. Takara was one of the first to re-introduce the Spoken Word in Honolulu to a room full of people—strangers included. Today, I count as long-time friends many of the folk I encountered for that first time during Takara's memorable performance at Pink's Garage so long ago.

What a tender but clever trickster Kathryn Takara was, revealing that poetry is not only accessible, but also transformative. Her poems release a wellspring of universal meaning. And her craft demonstrates its catalytic power in forging interconnectivity between the poetics and the reader.

With *Seasons in Haiku*, Takara beckons us once again to follow her down a pathway of purposeful communication cleared by poetic power. Only this time, she widens her focus beyond human interconnectivity to include human kinship with the four seasons of the natural world. For this 12th publication, she presents, for the first time, her selected haiku.

Haiku is the traditional Japanese poem of three lines and seventeen syllables, that, despite its brevity, offers bursts of imagery that are mesmerizing in their simplicity and largely based on the poet's first-hand experiences of nature, anchored in observations of the seasons.

In this collection, Takara's haiku are separated into four sections that correspond with the four seasons: Spring becomes SONGS; Summer becomes SHIMMER; Autumn becomes SHADOWS; and Winter becomes SOJOURN. Her haiku crisscrosses seamlessly between the visible and invisible layers of unfathomable phenomena that define each of these seasons. She deftly conveys these phases of nature as fleeting moments that elude the human yearning for permanence. With images that are pure distillations of sensorial experiences, she serves notice that the only sure thing about these seasonal moments is that they are transient and subject to change.

It is worth noting that Takara's haiku are set exclusively in Hawai`i. Thus, she debunks the stereotype of a seasonless tropical paradise which exists on postcards only. Instead, she captures the mesmerizing reality that there are few places in the world other than these islands where winter is synonymous with monster North Shore waves; or, where the coming of summer means some backyards are blanketed in heaps of overripe avocados and mangos; or, where the wide tropical vista is a vivid protean puzzle of species (our own included), reframed anew every day by spectacular shifts of light, wind, water, and fire, some in sync with the time of year and some not. Fire, for example, according to Takara's verses in this book, roars across all seasons, if one considers the peripatetic eruptions of live volcanoes on Hawai'i Island.

Moreover, she has an appealing knack for tying her clear-eyed depictions of nature's seasons to the seasons of human life. It may even be fair to say that Takara brings her innovative touch to repurposing the haiku for a timely foray into the relatively new territory of ecological poetry, or eco-poetry, as it has been dubbed. Eco-poetry strips away any illusion that we can afford to be mere observers of the natural world. Eco-poets instead deliver a clarion call to dwell in equanimity with all of creation in the interconnected lattices of life. Takara is on board with this ethos because she redefines this as a problem with a human face, underscoring the empowering perspective that if we caused the crisis, we can also fix it.

Takara's own story is never far from the surface in this volume of haiku. She reveals that her identity as a woman of Black and indigenous descent, means she is no stranger to the trauma of systemic injustice. While she is an impassioned champion of nature's seasonal cycles and the solace they offer in hard times, she does not write poetry to gloss over her own personal seasons rife with the pain of racial and gender discrimination, followed by her struggles with redemption, forgiveness, and perpetual discovery.

Seasons in Haiku resonates with many lessons that bring time-honored wisdom to bear on the uncertainties of our collective future. Today, during this tumultuous era, she once again draws on the old wisdom of haiku, affirming the timeless purpose of poetry in helping us to genuinely understand what we are only beginning to feel in a new day dawning

Thus, with her first volume of haiku, Kathryn Takara adds her voice to the rising chorus of other poets of color who not only speak truth to power, but also speak of the power they feel within themselves as they champion the natural beauty of the planet that is as inalienable as are human rights, and just as precious in the fight to protect resources, such as growth and transformation, that that are everyone's birthright.

TABLE OF CONTENTS

ACKNOWLEDGMENTS	ix
INTRODUCTION	xi
SONGS	1
TRACES	2
MESSAGES	3
BAMBOO	4
THE POND	5
SPRING FLINGS	6
BOUNCING BREEZE	7
MORNING STAGE	8
CAPRICIOUS CONDITIONS	9
REMEMBERING SPRING	10
AIR PLANTS	11
GARDEN DUTY	12
COUNTRY LIVING	13
HIDDEN INSPIRATION	14
TREMBLING MORNING	15
EVENING COMPANY	16
CROWN FLOWER	17
SOFT	18
MONARCH	19
OBSERVE SPRINGTIME	20

SACRED DANCING	21
LYRE OF ORPHEUS	22
RED SECRET	23
BEAUTY AND DANGER	24
GARDENIAS	25
MISSING PASSION	26
MALAEKAHANA BEACH	27
DINNER	28
SUBTLY	29
ORCHESTRA	30
CELESTIAL INFLUENCES	31
SHIMMER	33
EARLY MORNING FORAGING	34
FALLEN FRUITS	35
INVASION	36
CLINGING	37
STEPS TO HEAVEN	38
GOAT NEAR HI'IAKA BOULDER	39
KO'OLAU CASCADES	40
CHANNELING	41
UNPREDICTABLE	42
CALM	43
SUMMER SHOW	44

HAWAI`I SAILBOATS	45
BLOSSOMS	46
INVITATION	47
EVENING HUSH	48
COMFORT	49
MANGO SEASON	50
TROPICAL SURPRISE	51
EARLY WILT	52
WATERING	53
ASTRAL PEACE	54
TREASURE	55
JUNE DANCE	56
APPREHENSION	57
CLOUDY	58
FOREBODING	59
STING	60
HURRICANE	61
TANTRIC	62
FLOWING	63
VIBRATIONS	64
SHADOWS	65
PORTENDING PATTERN	66
TAROT THIEF	67

GROWTH	68
THE NORTH	69
TART JUICE	70
MORNING DOVES	71
COMPETITION	72
CANE SPIDER	73
WISH TO FLY	74
SYLPH GRACE	75
BOUNTY	76
SPICY	77
FEMME D'UN CERTAIN AGE	78
APHRODITE'S SECRETS	79
PASTEL TWILIGHT	80
A GOOD SEASON	81
DANGEROUS BEAUTY	82
FALLING	83
LAVA FIELDS	84
SKY LESSONS	85
CAUTION	86
BEWARE	87
LOST LEGENDS	88
SCENE IN SEPTEMBER	89
MORNING MYSTERIES	90

WISHES	91
EVENING	92
FADED FALLING	93
PROCESSES	94
RAKING PROMISES	95
SOJOURN	**97**
UPSTAIRS	98
OPEN SESAME	99
FORGOTTEN	100
AGED	101
MORNING TOILETTE	102
RESCUE	103
FOE	104
RELATIVITY	105
DANCING DEATH	106
WINTER GHOULS	107
DARKENING	108
DEEP VALLEY	109
ALCHEMY	110
BONFIRE	111
RESOLVE	112
OPENING	113
TIMING	114

CLARITY	115
WORDS	116
CONVERGENCES	117
CONCENTRIC	118
OPEN ARMS	119
COLOR CHART	120
SAGITTARIUS	121
CITRUS	122
WINTER'S HOPE	123
LIGHT MARVELS	124
PORTENTS	125
MYSTERY	126
ORIGAMI	127
EPILOGUE	129
ABOUT THE POET	135

SONGS

TRACES

Footprints on the grass
Enlightened path reveals cliffs
Ladders to be climbed.

MESSAGES

On spring wind I hear
My ancestors sing and dance
Listen to the words.

BAMBOO

Remember Papa
Strong growth around lotus pond
Embracing elders.

THE POND

Lily pads, bull frogs
Hungry fish throng through lotus
Colors, fragrance, sounds.

SPRING FLINGS

Pink plumeria
Bananas in back grow green
Jacaranda thrills.

BOUNCING BREEZE

Plumeria trees
Cardinal sings, wind tunes
In bouncing branches.

MORNING STAGE

Changing theater
Under trees, roosters, hens, chicks
Ripe mango opera.

CAPRICIOUS CONDITIONS

Flashes of sunlight
Predictable rain showers
Rainbows grace landscapes.

REMEMBERING SPRING

Lilac bush stretches
Tall to fragrant sun-filled deck
Bursting jubilance.

AIR PLANTS

Sprays of fresh orchids
Various bromeliads
Wondrous Spring surprise.

GARDEN DUTY

Bamboo shoots intrude
Papyrus spreads unbidden
Weeds choke young seedlings.

COUNTRY LIVING

Bird's delicate space
Away from urban bustle
Song creates wonder.

HIDDEN INSPIRATION

Day birds chirp sweetly
Hidden in naupaka bush
Inspire perfumed words.

TREMBLING MORNING

Sparrows, finches, doves
Mynahs, thrushes, cardinals
Inspiration trills.

EVENING COMPANY

Orange-breasted Shamas
Flash white tails and bright feathers
Crackle in bushes.

CROWN FLOWER

Watch crown flower leaves
Fat caterpillars devour
Transform in cocoon.

SOFT

Sudden burst of hope
From chrysalis of wonder
Soft butterfly wings.

MONARCH

Golden butterfly
In royal crown-flower bush
Becoming noble.

OBSERVE SPRINGTIME

Orange butterfly
Circuitous path of now
Follow bright floating.

SACRED DANCING

Mandala music
Aware possibilities
Mystical dancing.

LYRE OF ORPHEUS

Orpheus strums, sings
Lures Persephone to him
Cooing in Hades.

RED SECRET

10,000 petals
Strewn along the bridal path
Hide red centipede.

BEAUTY AND DANGER

Slippery grotto
Late spring orchids bloom nearby
Centipede slithers.

GARDENIAS

Jupiter displays
Baskets of bright abundance
Jovial bouquet.

MISSING PASSION

We held each other
Fleeting wild hot sensations
Love, I need you now!

MALAEKAHANA BEACH

Ukulele tune
Drifts above grove of sea grapes
Ocean roars welcome.

DINNER

He'e, ahi, squid
Shrimp, aku, parrot fish treats
Paradise bounty.

SUBTLY

Long fern fronds unfold
Stretch in morning sunshine warmth
Curl in evening chill.

ORCHESTRA

Jade lei hums beauty
Tiare strings allegro
Jasmine nocturne sooths.

CELESTIAL INFLUENCES

Luminescent moon
Bejeweled lavender sky
Silvers my brown skin.

EARLY MORNING FORAGING

Handsome red rooster
Promenades with three young hens
Seeking their breakfast.

FALLEN FRUITS

Russet wild rooster
Ventures close to large tied dog
Eats avocado.

INVASION

Lizards and geckos
Lounge quietly on white wall
Waiting for insects.

CLINGING

In banana stands
Liana vines tease tall trees
Grasping, holding on.

STEPS TO HEAVEN

Gold and rosy light
Cloud scape on the horizon
Suggests a stairway.

GOAT NEAR HI'IAKA BOULDER

Barely visible
Hind feet high on ocean cliff
Kualoa Point.

KO'OLAU CASCADES

Rainy mountain range
Waterfalls in crevices
Three hundred appear.

CHANNELING

Young albino goat
Sits high near burial cave
Seer of the waves.

UNPREDICTABLE

Blazing raging sun
Glazing on the summer sea
Passing rain surprise.

CALM

Breeze blows, calm ocean
Wave-whispers sing in wind-pines
Eat, love, sleep deeply.

SUMMER SHOW

Poet and painter
Planning out-of-pattern art
In the shade for lunch.

HAWAI`I SAILBOATS

Magic air shimmers
Friday regatta wind dance
Sunset ocean smiles.

BLOSSOMS

Happiness shimmers
The joy bird will not be still
Fragrant ginger floats.

INVITATION

Rose garden invites
Fragrance wafts from orange tree
Brave thorny kisses.

EVENING HUSH

A silent wish breathes
Temple Lake unveiled in June
There, a golden koi.

COMFORT

Tree mamas hover
Branches protecting lovers
From curious eyes.

MANGO SEASON

Tall wind rustles trees
Late summer fruits drop and crack
Deep golden sweetness.

TROPICAL SURPRISE

Orange blooms dazzle
Yellow butterflies flit high
Attention is green.

EARLY WILT

Tiare flower
Loses white fragrance in heat
Afternoon conquers.

WATERING

Thirsty plants wilted
Moon-light rain flows abundant
Beauty tomorrow.

ASTRAL PEACE

A walk through the clouds
On the moon, across the stars
Peace dream possible.

TREASURE

A person alone
Sits on a hot sandy beach
Finds beautiful shell.

JUNE DANCE

Aquarius bows
Dancers and water bearers
Green frogs sing fertile.

APPREHENSION

Swarms of summer storms
Camouflage latent violence
Suffering coming.

CLOUDY

Dark waifs in the sky
Giant sea turtles dive deep
Chilly emotions.

FOREBODING

Three black iwa birds
Ride the tall bright wind currents
Portend coming storm.

STING

Riding steeds of wind
Clouds spread, fearsome warriors
Sand scatters and stings.

HURRICANE

Sounds become muted
Stillness alerts in advance
Seething storm nearby.

TANTRIC

Tantric tension stirs
Reveals the dance to knowing.
Moon eats the lotus.

FLOWING

Libra and Ceres
Sisters in escape and dreams
Manifest changes.

VIBRATIONS

Listen to Nature
Hear a morphing symphony
Changing hidden notes.

PORTENDING PATTERN

Hazy sun sets north
Pierces red clouds, blood ocean
Eve before the storm.

TAROT THIEF

Furtive waterboy
Lifts bucket at the cistern
Looking stealthily.

GROWTH

Yesterday, a youth
Today, river channels dreams
Tomorrow, wisdom.

THE NORTH

The sky plum-purple
Rich harvest colors dissolve
Wind-strength from the north.

TART JUICE

Juggle the joy jar
Pick from up high, sweet grapefruits
Squeeze, drink, late harvest.

MORNING DOVES

Feeding time alert
Gray birds come, devour pet food
Coo on the railing.

COMPETITION

Honey Bee mother
Teaches her brood of ten chicks
How to fight for life.

CANE SPIDER

Large webless insect
Migrant from plantation fields
Jumps to surprise me!

WISH TO FLY

Butterflies galore
Skim tree tops, drink new nectars
Dance with each other.

SYLPH GRACE

Spirit of laughter
Near sylphs' translucent presence
Dainty, airy lights.

BOUNTY

Realm of young lovers
Harvest love's promised union
Treasure forgiveness.

SPICY

November hello
Tangerine and ginger air
Rain in profusion.

FEMME D'UN CERTAIN AGE

Passions lessening
Body changing, letting go
Not yet called the crone.

APHRODITE'S SECRETS

Scorpio sex gate
Surprise touching radiates
Sensuality.

PASTEL TWILIGHT

Taupe clouds, morph masters
Colors splash, apricot, peach
Adorn fading sky.

A GOOD SEASON

Baskets of harvest
Succulent fruits, veggies, nuts
Capricorns rejoice!

DANGEROUS BEAUTY

African snail crawls
Circles the collard green patch
Drops meningitis.

FALLING

Flowers from the tree
Fading pink plumeria
Disconnected deaths.

LAVA FIELDS

Pele's eruption
Lehua flowers tremble
Hot red imminent.

SKY LESSONS

Message from above
Night experience teaches
Listen! The silence.

CAUTION

Glassy swells beckon
Temptress of big waves disguised
Undercurrents strong.

BEWARE

A jewel legend
Darkness haunts the heartless night
No stash safe tonight.

LOST LEGENDS

Strands of words survive
Across veiled mists of insight
Sparkle, disappear.

SCENE IN SEPTEMBER

Through open windows
Brilliant radiance beckons
Red and gold hillside.

MORNING MYSTERIES

Veiled visions and dreams
Long strains of ancestral ghosts
Goats graze on lost hills.

WISHES

Bright coins in a pool
Dreamers tossing wishes true
Bottom shine soon fades.

EVENING

Northern lights reflect
Cause affects coded healing
Colorful magic.

FADED FALLING

Faded green dying
Leaves blow brown across driveway
Fall to burial.

PROCESSES

Spare me your pale sighs!
Leaves fade on the tree of life
Yet regenerate.

RAKING PROMISES

Plumeria trees
Lose their graceful tall shelter
Winter is coming.

SOJOURN

UPSTAIRS

Spectral rains surprise
Invade the upper locked room
Uncovered secrets.

OPEN SESAME

Invisible door
Clear beyond the empty room
Can I walk through it?

FORGOTTEN

Long screw on tile
Flashes like silver, shining
No place to burrow.

AGED

Old woman wanders
Whiskers camouflage her pain
Where is her family?

MORNING TOILETTE

Look in the mirror
New wrinkles loosening skin
More creams, breaths, stretching.

RESCUE

Pluck out silvered hairs
Catch judgment, negative thoughts
Rescue grace in age.

FOE

Time travels past hugs
Folds the past, bids the future
Open arm magic.

RELATIVITY

Parents are dying
Bonding broken evermore
Winter birds still sing.

DANCING DEATH

Ghosts convene dancing
Wispy robes move like high clouds
Osirus protects.

WINTER GHOULS

Ice cracks broken limbs
Skulls protrude just under skin
Graveside service planned.

DARKENING

Dark skin full of thorns
Pain wails without being heard
Such treacherous fear.

DEEP VALLEY

Soaring mountain ridge
Barrier to sun and moon
Cold gorge dark by day.

ALCHEMY

Dreams meet horizon
Catch manifestation barge
Dragon's holy fire.

BONFIRE

Farewell flames amaze
Blaze up to touch the black sky
Cold ashes remain.

RESOLVE

Where is the clear day
Deliverance from dark war
Syllables of peace?

OPENING

Seeker and empty
Trumps atheist and cynic
Winter bows to Spring.

TIMING

Daybreak splinters dark
Magical mysterious
Untold harmonies.

CLARITY

Birds sing perfect notes
Blend with dreams before long flights
Hidden harmonies.

WORDS

Light trilling of words
Transform across the seasons
Gold, silver, brass bells.

CONVERGENCES

Wind of pink promise
Convergence of soul and song
In bamboo knocking.

CONCENTRIC

It takes a strong breeze
To make the silent trees speak
The bark shines with life.

OPEN ARMS

Column of brightness
Rose up to welcome the day
Winter's daughter sighed.

COLOR CHART

Red, yellow, brown, blue
Bold colors transmitting strength
Strong black women live.

SAGITTARIUS

Painted on my toes
My mother liked the color
Sparkling sapphire blue.

CITRUS

Life squeezes our joy
Till it becomes nurturing
Lemon juice water.

WINTER'S HOPE

Filaments of light
Constellations, twinkling stars
Hope unveils promise.

LIGHT MARVELS

Nature's cycles stun
Suns, stars, planets unveil lights
Sea reflects the moon.

PORTENTS

Sun-streaked still waters
Clouds crouch on dark horizon
Watchful of changes.

MYSTERY

Belief in goodness
Hope perennial, a force
Blades of grass will grow.

ORIGAMI

Blossoms, petals, thorns
I arrange in a poem
Fragrance of my life.

EPILOGUE

Who am I?

I am the singer, and the song.
My surname is Japanese, but I am not.
I am a *femme d'un certain age*. I am a voice and a story.
I am multicultural.

I am a black woman married to an Asian man.
I am attracted to trans-cultural modes of expression:
aesthetics, simplicity, feelings of interconnectedness.
Respect and awareness are paths to pithy lessons.

I am an eco-poet
whose writings are greatly influenced by Nature.
I like to enchant, and to become enchanted
by the varied melodies of organic life,
by the mysterious levels of understanding,
by the magic and meanings of words, by love.

Why do I write Haiku?

I am a communicator, the singer and the song,
the teacher and the student.
I describe inner and outer manifestations.
I aspire to create calm, interest, curiosity, friction,
and growth.

The form of haiku attracts and speaks naturally to me,
for many reasons.
I grew up insulated from most southern violence
and prejudice,
tucked in the countryside of Macon County, Alabama,
surrounded by nature, towering trees and open green
spaces.

All around me
there were various rhythmic and lilting dialects
a kind of poetry in people and in Nature's voices.
I was inspired by knowledge and teaching
while living in a small Historically Black college community.
I was familiar with feelings of growth and freedom.

I am the singer and the song.

For the past five decades, I have lived in Hawaii,
in the verdant country, on a hillside
between old, inactive volcanic mountains,
with views of the ocean below.
Daily I observe the mysteries of life,
the cycles, seasons, synchronicities, and lessons
of Father Sky and Mother Earth
perennially present and accessible everywhere.

I am the singer and the song

I am a transmitter
to connect seasons to insights and wisdom,
inspired by singing beauty, songs of bountiful nature,
creative spirit, and abundant space.

What makes a Haiku?

Haiku is a traditional form
written in 3 lines and 17 syllables (5 x 7 x 5).
The poet renders a powerful sketch in haiku:
the short refrain, the evocation of mind pictures,
the many-tiered meanings possible in one word or scene,
the use of metaphors, the alliteration, all in small spaces.
This form is a personal challenge for me to simplify my style.
It is the discipline of writing sparsely with few words,
a shifting from a concrete, clear visual image
to an abstract connection.

What is a Haiku?

Haiku exposes the intricacies of Nature.
It is the juxtaposition of difference and similarity
to create an understandable, relatable connection.
Haiku is often seasonal, a word witness of correspondences
with a focus on scenery
and not on human action and activities.
There seems to be a level of separation from the ego, the "I".

Haiku is full of allusions
to the five senses,
to metaphorical sleep and awakening,
to organic and inorganic life.

A haiku can be like a temple, a sanctuary,
a sacred poem about place.
It can reveal a prison of mediocrity
and blind habits of seeing.
It can open metaphorical closed windows and roads
to new levels of being and understanding.

It can offer the possibility of travel
(virtual and real) and of adventure.
Haiku can create an unforeseen escape
from the ordinariness of life.
A haiku can offer a shock.

Haiku is the poet's emotional and philosophical response
to seasons, to Nature, to the processes and conditions of life,
observed closely and articulated in sparse details.
It can connect beauty, sensations, and colors
with elucidation, imagination, revelation, and dreams.

The seasons are Nature's breathing cycles
of perennial passages.
The poet-observer can find parallels
with human growth, obstacles, struggles to survive
and regeneration.
Haiku may reflect the inevitable processes of life.

Haiku is

Haiku is an opening of consciousness,
a form of connectivity through word pictures.
It evokes a conscience to protect and support
the land and Nature's manifestations.

Haiku is a shout of celebration
Or a dirge of nostalgia and loss.
It is the song of springtime and love,
the shimmer of summer and growth,
the shadowy autumn of harvest and even of corruption,
the indigo winter sojourn of inactivity, reflection,
death and transformation.

Haiku is transcendent,
a spiral of awakening for the writer and the audience.
Haiku is movement, the subtle or blatant changes
between stillness and motion, light and darkness.

Haiku is relaxing yet provocative,
comforting yet disturbing.
Usually, haiku evokes new levels of attention,

Haiku is a gift,
a small package of quiet peace, and new connections
Haiku can point the way to a possible evolution
of mysterious and transformative healing.
. Haiku is instructive.

I am

a writer with a message,
a singer with a song.

Kathryn Takara

ABOUT THE POET

Kathryn Waddell Takara, PhD is a renaissance woman and the author of eleven previous books.

She is an Historian, Political Scientist, philosophical Afrofuturist, Eco-poet, researcher, public scholar, and writer of scholarly articles.

Takara has been awarded The American Book Award, The national History Makers Award, Black Futures Award, NAACP Life Time Achievement Award, and she was knighted into the Orthodox Order of St. John (OOSJ). Recently, she has been interviewed about her research by national, international and local press on the inventor Alice Augusta Ball, and the little known historical presence of early Blacks in Hawai'i.

In the period of Covid 19 (2020-21), she has published 4 books through her press, Pacific Raven Press LLC, completed several podcasts, co-produced a jazz night in Honolulu featuring the music of Thelonius Monk, has given presentations at the UN/NGO for OOSJ ("Cry Children of the World: The Work and Meaning of Knighthood"), lectured on seven contemporary black artists and the Black Arts Movement for the Honolulu Museum, and performed in several poetry readings that include "Black Fire This Time," "Wake Up America," and multiple Martin Luther King Day, Black History and Women's months events. Takara curated a public library Black History month exhibit in 2020 that featured local artists.

Currently, she is an acting consultant for several creative projects, including a film on Rev. Dr. Martin Luther King Jr.'s early visit to Hawai'i.

On a personal note, Kathryn Takara was born in Tuskegee, Alabama, and has been a Hawai'i resident since 1968. She carries an MA French from UC Berkeley, and a PhD in Political Science from the University of Hawai'i at Mānoa and she was the recipient of 2 Fulbright fellowships. She studied at the University of Bordeaux and was a summer lecturer at the University of Qingdao, China (1995-2016), and several other small universities in Beijing.

As a former French instructor and retired Professor of Black Studies at the University of Hawai'i Mānoa, Takara now has more time to be an entrepreneur, writer, and editor as well as a committed world traveler, public scholar, spiritual teacher, community activist, gardener, wife, mother, and grandmother.

www.ingramcontent.com/pod-product-compliance
Lightning Source LLC
LaVergne TN
LVHW021948060526
838200LV00043B/1954